We Like to
Play

by Barrie Wade and Melanie Sharp

We like to play

with puppets.

We like to play

with water.

We like to play

with sand.

We like to play

with bricks.

We like to play

with paint.

We like to play

with clay.

We like to play

with shapes.

We like to play

with glitter.

We like to play

with teddy.

Story trail

Start

Start at the beginning of the story trail. Ask your child to retell the story in their own words, pointing to each picture in turn to recall the sequence of events.

Independent Reading

This series is designed to provide an opportunity for your child to read on their own. These notes are written for you to help your child choose a book and to read it independently.

In school, your child's teacher will often be using reading books which have been banded to support the process of learning to read. Use the book band colour your child is reading in school to help you make a good choice. *We Like to Play* is a good choice for children reading at Pink 1b in their classroom to read independently.

The aim of independent reading is to read this book with ease, so that your child enjoys the story and relates it to their own experiences.

About the book

In this book, the children have lots of fun playing with all sorts of things, from puppets to glitter. But teddy never gets to join in. Then, at last, they play with teddy.

Before reading

Help your child to learn how to make good choices by asking: "Why did you choose this book? Why do you think you will enjoy it?" Support your child to think about what they already know about the story context. Look at the cover together and ask: "What do you think the book will be about?" Read the title aloud and ask: "Do you think they like playing?" Then say, "I wonder if they will play with other things in their classroom?"

Remind your child that they can try to sound out the letters to make a word if they get stuck.

Decide together whether your child will read the story independently or read it aloud to you. When books are short, as at Pink 1b, your child may wish to do both!

During reading

If reading aloud, support your child if they hesitate or ask for help by telling the word. Remind your child of what they know and what they can do independently.

If reading to themselves, remind your child that they can come and ask for your help if stuck.

After reading

Support comprehension by asking your child to tell you about the book. Help your child think about the messages in the book that go beyond the story and ask: "Do you think the children enjoyed playing with teddy? Why do you think that?"

Give your child a chance to respond to the story: "Did you have a favourite part? Why do you like that part?"

Use the story trail to encourage your child to retell the story in the right sequence, in their own words.

Extending learning

Help your child extend the story structure by using the same sentence pattern and changing the context. "What else could the children play with? Let's change the story so that the children are playing somewhere else. Let's imagine they went to the park. They might go on the see-saw: We like to play on the see-saw. Now you think of what they might like at the park."

On a few of the pages, check your child can finger point accurately by asking them to show you how they kept their place in the print by tracking from word to word.

Help your child to use letter information by asking them to find the interest word on each page by using the first letter. For example: "Which word is 'water'? How do you know it is that word?"

Franklin Watts
First published in Great Britain in 2017
by The Watts Publishing Group

Series Editors: Jackie Hamley and Melanie Palmer
Series Advisors: Dr Sue Bodman and Glen Franklin
Series Designer: Peter Scoulding

A CIP catalogue record for this book is
available from the British Library.

ISBN 978 1 4451 5421 3 (hbk)
ISBN 978 1 4451 5422 0 (pbk)

Printed in China

Franklin Watts
An imprint of
Hachette Children's Group
Part of The Watts Publishing Group
Carmelite House
50 Victoria Embankment
London EC4Y 0DZ

An Hachette UK Company
www.hachette.co.uk

www.franklinwatts.co.uk

FSC
www.fsc.org
MIX
Paper from
responsible sources
FSC® C104740